Deirdre of the Sorrows

J. M. Synge

Contents

DEIRDRE OF THE SORROWS By J. M. SYNGE 7
ACT I. 8
ACT II. 33
ACT III. 52

DEIRDRE OF THE SORROWS

BY
J. M. Synge

DEIRDRE OF THE SORROWS
By J. M. SYNGE

PERSONS IN THE PLAY

LAVARCHAM, Deirdre's nurse

OLD WOMAN, Lavarcham's servant

OWEN, Conchubor's attendant and spy

CONCHUBOR, High King of Ulster

FERGUS, Conchubor's friend

DEIRDRE

NAISI, Deirdre's lover

AINNLE, Naisi's brother

ARDAN, Naisi's brother

TWO SOLDIERS

ACT I.

Lavarcham's house
on Slieve Fuadh.

    Lavarcham's house on Slieve Fuadh. There is a door to inner room on the left, and a door to open air on the right. Window at back and a frame with a half-finished piece of tapestry. There are also a large press and heavy oak chest near the back wall. The place is neat and clean but bare. Lavarcham, woman of fifty, is working at tapestry frame. Old Woman comes in from left.
    OLD WOMAN. She hasn't come yet, is it, and it falling to the night?
    LAVARCHAM. She has not. . . (Concealing her anxiety.) It's dark with the clouds are coming from the west and south, but it isn't later than the common.
    OLD WOMAN. It's later, surely, and I hear tell the Sons of Usna, Naisi and his brothers, are above chasing hares for two days or three, and the same awhile since when the moon was full.
    LAVARCHAM -- more anxiously. -- The

gods send they don't set eyes on her -- (with a sign of helplessness) yet if they do itself, it wasn't my wish brought them or could send them away.

OLD WOMAN -- reprovingly. -- If it wasn't, you'd do well to keep a check on her, and she turning a woman that was meant to be a queen.

LAVARCHAM. Who'd check her like was meant to have her pleasure only, the way if there were no warnings told about her you'd see troubles coming when an old king is taking her, and she without a thought but for her beauty and to be straying the hills.

OLD WOMAN. The gods help the lot of us. . . . Shouldn't she be well pleased getting the like of Conchubor, and he middling settled in his years itself? I don't know what he wanted putting her this wild place to be breaking her in, or putting myself to be roasting her supper and she with no patience for her food at all. [She looks out.

LAVARCHAM. Is she coming from the glen?

OLD WOMAN. She is not. But whisht -- there's two men leaving the furze -- (crying out) it's Conchubor and Fergus along with him. Conchubor'll be in a blue stew this night and herself abroad.

LAVARCHAM -- settling room hastily. -- Are they close by?

OLD WOMAN. Crossing the stream, and there's herself on the hillside with a load of twigs. Will I run out and put her in order before they'll set eyes on her at all?

LAVARCHAM. You will not. Would you have him see you, and he a man would be jealous of a hawk would fly between her and the rising sun. (She looks out.) Go up to the hearth and be as busy as if you hadn't seen them at all.

OLD WOMAN -- sitting down to polish vessel. -- There'll be trouble this night, for he should be in his tempers from the way he's stepping out, and he swinging his hands.

LAVARCHAM -- wearied with the whole matter. -- It'd be best of all, maybe, if he got in tempers with herself, and made an end quickly, for I'm in a poor way between the pair of them (going back to tapestry frame.) There they are now at the door.

    [Conchubor and Fergus come in.

CONCHUBOR AND FERGUS. The gods save you.

LAVARCHAM -- getting up and courtesying. -- The gods save and keep you kindly, and stand between you and all harm for ever.

CONCHUBOR -- looking around. -- Where is Deirdre?

LAVARCHAM -- trying to speak with indifference. -- Abroad upon Slieve Fuadh. She does be all times straying around picking flowers or nuts, or sticks itself; but so long as she's gathering new life I've a right not to heed her, I'm thinking, and she taking her will.

    [Fergus talks to Old Woman.

CONCHUBOR -- stiffly. -- A night with thunder coming is no night to be abroad.

LAVARCHAM -- more uneasily. -- She's used to every track and pathway, and the lightning itself wouldn't let down its flame to singe the beauty of her like.

FERGUS -- cheerfully. -- She's right, Conchubor, and let you sit down and take your ease, (he takes a wallet from under his cloak) and I'll count out what we've brought, and put it in the presses within.

[He goes into the inner room with the Old Woman.

CONCHUBOR -- sitting down and looking about. -- Where are the mats and hangings and the silver skillets I sent up for Deirdre?

LAVARCHAM. The mats and hangings are in this press, Conchubor. She wouldn't wish to be soiling them, she said, running out and in with mud and grasses on her feet, and it raining since the night of Samhain. The silver skillets and the golden cups we have beyond locked in the chest.

CONCHUBOR. Bring them out and use them from this day.

LAVARCHAM. We'll do it, Conchubor.

CONCHUBOR -- getting up and going to frame. -- Is this hers?

LAVARCHAM -- pleased to speak of it. -- It is, Conchubor. All say there isn't her match at fancying figures and throwing purple upon crimson, and she edging them all times with her greens and gold.

CONCHUBOR -- a little uneasily. -- Is she keeping wise and busy since I passed before, and growing ready for her life in Emain?

LAVARCHAM -- dryly. -- That is a question will give small pleasure to yourself or me. (Making up her mind to speak out.) If it's the truth I'll tell you, she's growing too wise to marry a big king and she a score only. Let you not be taking it bad, Conchubor, but you'll get little good seeing her this night, for with all my talking it's wilfuller she's growing these two months or three.

CONCHUBOR -- severely, but relieved things are no worse. -- Isn't it a poor thing you're doing so little to school her to meet what is to come?

LAVARCHAM. I'm after serving you two score of years, and I'll tell you this night, Conchubor, she's little call to mind an old woman when she has the birds to school her, and the pools in the rivers where she goes bathing in the sun. I'll tell you if you seen her that time, with her white skin, and her red lips, and the blue water and the ferns about her, you'd know, maybe, and you greedy itself, it wasn't for your like she was born at all.

CONCHUBOR. It's little I heed for what she was born; she'll be my comrade, surely.

[He examines her workbox.

LAVARCHAM -- sinking into sadness again. -- I'm in dread so they were right saying she'd bring destruction on the world, for it's a poor thing when you see a settled man putting the love he has for a young child, and the love he has for a full woman, on a girl the like of her; and it's a poor thing, Conchubor, to see a High King, the way you are this day, prying after her needles and numbering her lines of thread.

CONCHUBOR -- getting up. -- Let you not be talking too far and you old itself. (Walks across room and back.) Does she know the troubles are foretold?

LAVARCHAM -- in the tone of the earlier talk. -- I'm after telling her one time and another, but I'd do as well speaking to a lamb of ten weeks and it racing the hills. . . . It's not the dread of death or troubles that would tame her like.

CONCHUBOR -- he looks out. -- She's coming now, and let you walk in and keep Fergus till I speak with her a while.

LAVARCHAM -- going left. -- If I'm after vexing you itself, it'd be best you weren't taking her hasty or scolding her at all.

CONCHUBOR -- very stiffly. -- I've no call to. I'm well pleased she's light and airy.

LAVARCHAM -- offended at his tone. -- Well pleased is it? (With a snort of irony) It's a queer thing the way the likes of me do be telling the truth, and the wise are lying all times.

[She goes into room on left. Conchubor arranges himself before a mirror for a moment, then goes a little to the left and waits. Deirdre comes in poorly dressed, with a little bag and a bundle of twigs in her arms. She is astonished for a moment when she sees Conchubor; then she makes a courtesy to him, and goes to the hearth without any embarrassment.

CONCHUBOR. The gods save you, Deirdre. I have come up bringing you rings and jewels from Emain Macha.

DEIRDRE. The gods save you.

CONCHUBOR. What have you brought from the hills?

DEIRDRE -- quite self-possessed. -- A bag of nuts, and twigs for our fires at the dawn of day.

CONCHUBOR -- showing annoyance in spite of himself. -- And it's that way you're picking up the manners will fit you to be Queen of Ulster?

DEIRDRE -- made a little defiant by his tone. -- I have no wish to be a queen.

CONCHUBOR -- almost sneeringly. -- You'd wish to be dressing in your duns and grey, and you herding your geese or driving your calves to their shed -- like the common lot scattered in the glens.

DEIRDRE -- very defiant. -- I would not, Conchubor. (She goes to tapestry and begins to work.) A girl born the way I'm born is more likely to wish for a mate who'd be her likeness.... A man with his hair like the raven, maybe, and his skin like the snow and his lips like blood spilt on it.

CONCHUBOR -- sees his mistake, and after a moment takes a flattering tone, looking at her work. -- Whatever you wish, there's no queen but would be well pleased to have your skill at choosing colours and making pictures on the cloth. (Looking closely.) What is it you're figuring?

DEIRDRE -- deliberately. -- Three young men and they chasing in the green gap of a wood.

CONCHUBOR -- now almost pleading. -- It's soon you'll have dogs with silver chains to be chasing in the woods of Emain, for I have white hounds rearing up for you, and grey horses, that I've chosen from the finest in Ulster and Britain and Gaul.

DEIRDRE -- unmoved as before. -- I've heard tell, in Ulster and Britain and Gaul, Naisi and his brothers have no match and they chasing in the woods.

CONCHUBOR -- very gravely. -- Isn't it a strange thing you'd be talking of Naisi and his brothers, or figuring them either, when you know the things that are foretold about themselves and you? Yet you've little knowledge, and I'd do wrong taking it bad when it'll be my share from this out to keep you the way you'll have little call to trouble for knowledge, or its want either.

DEIRDRE. Yourself should be wise, surely.

CONCHUBOR. The like of me has a store of knowledge that's a weight and terror.

It's for that we do choose out the like of yourself that are young and glad only. . . . I'm thinking you are gay and lively each day in the year?

DEIRDRE. I don't know if that's true, Conchubor. There are lonesome days and bad nights in this place like another.

CONCHUBOR. You should have as few sad days, I'm thinking, as I have glad and good ones.

DEIRDRE. What is it has you that way ever coming this place, when you'd hear the old woman saying a good child's as happy as a king?

CONCHUBOR. How would I be happy seeing age coming on me each year, when the dry leaves are blowing back and forward at the gate of Emain? And yet this last while I'm saying out, when I see the furze breaking and the daws sitting two and two on ash-trees by the duns of Emain, Deirdre's a year nearer her full age when she'll be my mate and comrade and then I'm glad surely.

DEIRDRE -- almost to herself. -- I will not be your mate in Emain.

CONCHUBOR -- not heeding her. -- It's there you'll be proud and happy and you'll learn that, if young men are great hunters, yet it's with the like of myself you'll find a knowledge of what is priceless in your own like. What we all need is a place is safe and splendid, and it's that you'll get in Emain in two days or three.

DEIRDRE -- aghast. -- Two days!

CONCHUBOR. I have the rooms ready, and in a little while you'll be brought down there, to be my queen and queen of the five parts of Ireland.

DEIRDRE -- standing up frightened and pleading. -- I'd liefer stay this place, Conchubor.... Leave me this place, where I'm well used to the tracks and pathways and the people of the glens.... It's for this life I'm born, surely.

CONCHUBOR. You'll be happier and greater with myself in Emain. It is I will be your comrade, and will stand between you and the great troubles are foretold.

DEIRDRE. I will not be your queen in Emain when it's my pleasure to be having my freedom on the edges of the hills.

CONCHUBOR. It's my wish to have you quickly; I'm sick and weary thinking of the day you'll be brought down to me, and seeing you walking into my big, empty halls. I've made all sure to have you, and yet all said there's a fear in the back of my mind I'd miss you and have great troubles in the end. It's for that, Deirdre, I'm praying that you'll come quickly; and you may take the word of a man has no lies, you'll not find, with any other, the like of what I'm bringing you in wildness and confusion in my own mind.

DEIRDRE. I cannot go, Conchubor.

CONCHUBOR -- taking a triumphant tone. -- It is my pleasure to have you, and I a man is waiting a long while on the throne of Ulster. Wouldn't you liefer be my comrade, growing up the like of Emer and Maeve, than to be in this place and you a child always?

DEIRDRE. You don't know me and you'd have little joy taking me, Conchubor. ... I'm a long while watching the days getting a great speed passing me by. I'm too long taking my will, and it's that way I'll be living always.

CONCHUBOR -- dryly. -- Call Fergus to come with me. This is your last night upon Slieve Fuadh.

DEIRDRE -- now pleadingly. -- Leave me a short space longer, Conchubor. Isn't it a poor thing I should be hastened away, when all these troubles are foretold? Leave me a year, Conchubor; it isn't much I'm asking.

CONCHUBOR. It's much to have me two score and two weeks waiting for your voice in Emain, and you in this place growing lonesome and shy. I'm a ripe man and in great love, and yet, Deirdre, I'm the King of Ulster. (He gets up.) I'll call Fergus, and we'll make Emain ready in the morning.

[He goes towards door on left.

DEIRDRE -- clinging to him. -- Do not call him, Conchubor.... Promise me a year of quiet.... It's one year I'm asking only.

CONCHUBOR. You'd be asking a year next year, and the years that follow. (Calling.) Fergus! Fergus! (To Deirdre.) Young girls are slow always; it is their lovers

that must say the word. (Calling.) Fergus!
  [Deirdre springs away from him as
    Fergus comes in with Lavarcham and
    the Old Woman.
CONCHUBOR -- to Fergus. -- There is a storm coming, and we'd best be going to our people when the night is young.

FERGUS -- cheerfully. -- The gods shield you, Deirdre. (To Conchubor.) We're late already, and it's no work the High King to be slipping on stepping-stones and hilly pathways when the floods are rising with the rain.
    [He helps Conchubor into his cloak.
CONCHUBOR -- glad that he has made his decision -- to Lavarcham. -- Keep your rules a few days longer, and you'll be brought down to Emain, you and Deirdre with you.

LAVARCHAM -- obediently. -- Your rules are kept always.

CONCHUBOR. The gods shield you.
  [He goes out with Fergus. Old Woman
    bolts door.
LAVARCHAM -- looking at Deirdre, who has covered her face. -- Wasn't I saying you'd do it? You've brought your marriage a sight nearer not heeding those are wiser than yourself.

DEIRDRE -- with agitation. -- It wasn't I did it. Will you take me from this place, Lavarcham, and keep me safe in the hills?

LAVARCHAM. He'd have us tracked in the half of a day, and then you'd be his queen in spite of you, and I and mine would be destroyed for ever.

DEIRDRE -- terrified with the reality that is before her. -- Are there none can go against Conchubor?

LAVARCHAM. Maeve of Connaught only, and those that are her like.

DEIRDRE. Would Fergus go against him?

LAVARCHAM. He would, maybe, and his temper roused.

DEIRDRE -- in a lower voice with sudden excitement. -- Would Naisi and his brothers?

LAVARCHAM -- impatiently. -- Let you not be dwelling on Naisi and his brothers. . . . In the end of all there is none can go against Conchubor, and it's folly that we're talking, for if any went against Conchubor it's sorrow he'd earn and the shortening of his day of life.

>   [She turns away, and Deirdre stands up stiff with excitement and goes and looks out of the window.

DEIRDRE. Are the stepping-stones flooding, Lavarcham? Will the night be stormy in the hills?

LAVARCHAM -- looking at her curiously. The stepping-stones are flooding, surely, and the night will be the worst, I'm thinking, we've seen these years gone by.

DEIRDRE -- tearing open the press and pulling out clothes and tapestries. -- Lay these mats and hangings by the windows, and at the tables for our feet, and take out the skillets of silver, and the golden cups we have, and our two flasks of wine.

LAVARCHAM. What ails you?

DEIRDRE -- gathering up a dress. -- Lay them out quickly, Lavarcham, we've no call dawdling this night. Lay them out quickly; I'm going into the room to put on the rich dresses and jewels have been sent from Emain.

LAVARCHAM. Putting on dresses at this hour, and it dark and drenching with the weight of rain! Are you away in your head?

DEIRDRE -- gathering her things together with an outburst of excitement. -- I will dress like Emer in Dundealgan, or Maeve in her house in Connaught. If Conchubor'll make me a queen, I'll have the right of a queen who is a master, taking her own choice and making a stir to the edges of the seas. . . . Lay out your mats and hangings where I can stand this night and look about me. Lay out the skins of the rams of Connaught and of the goats of the west. I will not be a child or plaything; I'll put on my robes that are the richest, for I will not be brought down to Emain as Cuchulain brings his horse to the yoke, or Conall Cearneach puts his shield upon his arm; and maybe from this day I will turn the men of Ireland like a wind blowing on the heath.

> [She goes into room. Lavarcham and Old Woman look at each other, then the Old Woman goes over, looks in at Deirdre through chink of the door, and then closes it carefully.

OLD WOMAN -- in a frightened whisper. -- She's thrown off the rags she had about her, and there she is in her skin; she's putting her hair in shiny twists. Is she raving, Lavarcham, or has she a good right turning to a queen like Maeve?

LAVARCHAM -- putting up hanging very anxiously. -- It's more than raving's in her mind, or I'm the more astray; and yet she's as good a right as another, maybe, having her pleasure, though she'd spoil the world.

OLD WOMAN -- helping her. -- Be quick before she'll come back.... Who'd have thought we'd run before her, and she so quiet till to-night. Will the High King get the better of her, Lavarcham? If I was Conchubor, I wouldn't marry with her like at all.

LAVARCHAM. Hang that by the window. That should please her, surely. When all's said, it's her like will be the master till the end of time.

OLD WOMAN -- at the window. -- There's a mountain of blackness in the sky, and the greatest rain falling has been these long years on the earth. The gods help Conchubor. He'll be a sorry man this night, reaching his dun, and he with all his spirits, thinking to himself he'll be putting his arms around her in two days or three.

LAVARCHAM. It's more than Conchubor'll be sick and sorry, I'm thinking, before this story is told to the end.

[Loud knocking on door at the right.

LAVARCHAM -- startled. -- Who is that?

NAISI -- outside. -- Naisi and his brothers.

LAVARCHAM. We are lonely women. What is it you're wanting in the blackness of the night?

NAISI. We met a young girl in the woods who told us we might shelter this place if the rivers rose on the pathways and the floods gathered from the butt of the hills.

[Old Woman clasps her hands in horror.

LAVARCHAM -- with great alarm. -- You cannot come in. . . . There is no one let in here, and no young girl with us.

NAISI. Let us in from the great storm. Let us in and we will go further when the cloud will rise.

LAVARCHAM. Go round east to the shed and you'll have shelter. You cannot come in.

NAISI -- knocking loudly. -- Open the door or we will burst it. (The door is shaken.)

OLD WOMAN -- in a timid whisper. -- Let them in, and keep Deirdre in her room to-night.

AINNLE AND ARDAN -- outside. -- Open! Open!

LAVARCHAM -- to Old Woman. -- Go in and keep her.

OLD WOMAN. I couldn't keep her. I've no hold on her. Go in yourself and I will free the door.

LAVARCHAM. I must stay and turn them out. (She pulls her hair and cloak over her face.) Go in and keep her.

OLD WOMAN. The gods help us.
  [She runs into the inner room.

VOICES. Open!

LAVARCHAM -- opening the door. -- Come in then and ill-luck if you'll have it so.

  [Naisi and Ainnle and Ardan come in
    and look round with astonishment.

NAISI. It's a rich man has this place, and no herd at all.

LAVARCHAM -- sitting down with her head half covered. -- It is not, and you'd best be going quickly.

NAISI -- hilariously, shaking rain from his clothes. -- When we've had the pick of luck finding princely comfort in the darkness of the night! Some rich man of Ulster should come here and he chasing in the woods. May we drink? (He takes up flask.) Whose wine is this that we may drink his health?

LAVARCHAM. It's no one's that you've call to know.

NAISI. Your own health then and length of life. (Pouring out wine for the three. They drink.)

LAVARCHAM -- very crossly. -- You're great boys taking a welcome where it isn't given, and asking questions where you've no call to. . . . If you'd a quiet place settled up to be playing yourself, maybe, with a gentle queen, what'd you think of young men prying around and carrying tales? When I was a bit of a girl the big men of Ulster had better manners, and they the like of your three selves, in the top folly of youth. That'll be a story to tell out in Tara that Naisi is a tippler and stealer, and Ainnle the drawer of a stranger's cork.

 NAISI -- quite cheerfully, sitting down beside her. -- At your age you should know there are nights when a king like Conchubor will spit upon his arm ring, and queens will stick their tongues out at the rising moon. We're that way this night, and it's not wine we're asking only. Where is the young girl told us we might shelter here?

 LAVARCHAM. Asking me you'd be? We're decent people, and I wouldn't put you tracking a young girl, not if you gave me the gold clasp you have hanging on your coat.

 NAISI -- giving it to her. -- Where is she?

 LAVARCHAM -- in confidential whisper, putting her hand on his arm. -- Let you walk back into the hills and turn up by the second cnuceen where there are three together. You'll see a path running on the rocks and then you'll hear the dogs barking in the houses, and their noise will guide you till you come to a bit of cabin at the foot of an ash-tree. It's there there is a young and flighty girl that I'm thinking is the one you've seen.

 NAISI -- hilariously. -- Here's health, then, to herself and you!

 ARDAN. Here's to the years when you were young as she!

 AINNLE -- in a frightened whisper. --

Naisi!

> [Naisi looks up and Ainnle beckons to him. He goes over and Ainnle points to something on the golden mug he holds in his hand.

NAISI -- looking at it in astonishment. -- This is the High King's. . . . I see his mark on the rim. Does Conchubor come lodging here?

LAVARCHAM -- jumping up with extreme annoyance. -- Who says it's Conchubor's? How dare young fools the like of you -- (speaking with vehement insolence) come prying around, running the world into troubles for some slip of a girl? What brings you this place straying from Emain? (Very bitterly.) Though you think, maybe, young men can do their fill of foolery and there is none to blame them.

NAISI -- very soberly. -- Is the rain easing?

ARDAN. The clouds are breaking. . . . I can see Orion in the gap of the glen.

NAISI -- still cheerfully. -- Open the door and we'll go forward to the little cabin between the ash-tree and the rocks. Lift the bolt and pull it.

> [Deirdre comes in on left royally dressed and very beautiful. She stands for a moment, and then as the door opens she calls softly.

DEIRDRE. Naisi! Do not leave me, Naisi. I am Deirdre of the Sorrows.

NAISI -- transfixed with amazement. --

And it is you who go around in the woods making the thrushes bear a grudge against the heavens for the sweetness of your voice singing.

DEIRDRE. It is with me you've spoken, surely. (To Lavarcham and Old Woman.) Take Ainnle and Ardan, these two princes, into the little hut where we eat, and serve them with what is best and sweetest. I have many thing for Naisi only.

LAVARCHAM -- overawed by her tone. -- I will do it, and I ask their pardon. I have fooled them here.

DEIRDRE -- to Ainnle and Ardan. -- Do not take it badly that I am asking you to walk into our hut for a little. You will have a supper that is cooked by the cook of Conchubor, and Lavarcham will tell you stories of Maeve and Nessa and Rogh.

AINNLE. We'll ask Lavarcham to tell us stories of yourself, and with that we'll be well pleased to be doing your wish.

[They all go out except Deirdre and Naisi.

DEIRDRE -- sitting in the high chair in the centre. -- Come to this stool, Naisi (pointing to the stool). If it's low itself the High King would sooner be on it this night than on the throne of Emain Macha.

NAISI -- sitting down. -- You are Fedlimid's daughter that Conchubor has walled up from all the men of Ulster.

DEIRDRE. Do many know what is foretold, that Deirdre will be the ruin of the Sons of Usna, and have a little grave by herself, and a story will be told for ever?

NAISI. It's a long while men have been talking of Deirdre, the child who had all gifts, and the beauty that has no equal; there are many know it, and there are kings would give a great price to be in my place this night and you grown to a queen.

DEIRDRE. It isn't many I'd call, Naisi. . . . I was in the woods at the full moon and I heard a voice singing. Then I gathered up my skirts, and I ran on a little path I have to the verge of a rock, and I saw you pass by underneath, in your crimson cloak, singing a song, and you standing out beyond your brothers are called the Plower of Ireland.

NAISI. It's for that you called us in the dusk?

DEIRDRE -- in a low voice. -- Since that, Naisi, I have been one time the like of a ewe looking for a lamb that had been taken away from her, and one time seeing new gold on the stars, and a new face on the moon, and all times dreading Emain.

NAISI -- pulling himself together and beginning to draw back a little. -- Yet it should be a lonesome thing to be in this place and you born for great company.

DEIRDRE -- softly. -- This night I have the best company in the whole world.

NAISI -- still a little formally. -- It is I who have the best company, for when you're queen in Emain you will have none to be your match or fellow.

DEIRDRE. I will not be queen in Emain.

NAISI. Conchubor has made an oath you will, surely.

DEIRDRE. It's for that maybe I'm called Deirdre, the girl of many sorrows . . . for it's a sweet life you and I could have, Naisi. . . . . It should be a sweet thing to have what is best and richest, if it's for a short space only.

NAISI -- very distressed. -- And we've a short space only to be triumphant and brave.

DEIRDRE. You must not go, Naisi, and leave me to the High King, a man is aging in his dun, with his crowds round him, and his silver and gold. (More quickly.) I will not live to be shut up in Emain, and wouldn't we do well paying, Naisi, with silence and a near death. (She stands up and walks away from him.) I'm a long while in the woods with my own self, and I'm in little dread of death, and it earned with riches would make the sun red with envy, and he going up the heavens; and the moon pale and lonesome, and she wasting away. (She comes to him and puts her hands on his shoulders.) Isn't it a small thing is foretold about the ruin of ourselves, Naisi, when all men have age coming and great ruin in the end?

NAISI. Yet it's a poor thing it's I should bring you to a tale of blood and broken bodies, and the filth of the grave. . . . Wouldn't we do well to wait, Deirdre, and I each twilight meeting you on the sides of the hills?

DEIRDRE -- despondently. -- His messengers are coming.

NAISI. Messengers are coming?

DEIRDRE. To-morrow morning or the next, surely.

NAISI. Then we'll go away. It isn't I will give your like to Conchubor, not if the grave was dug to be my lodging when a week was by. (He looks out.) The stars are out, Deirdre, and let you come with me quickly, for it is the stars will be our lamps many nights and we abroad in Alban, and taking our journeys among the little islands in the sea. There has never been the like of the joy we'll have, Deirdre, you and I, having our fill of love at the evening and the morning till the sun is high.

DEIRDRE. And yet I'm in dread leaving this place, where I have lived always. Won't I be lonesome and I thinking on the little hill beyond, and the apple-trees do be budding in the spring-time by the post of the door? (A little shaken by what has passed.) Won't I be in great dread to bring you to destruction, Naisi, and you so happy and young?

NAISI. Are you thinking I'd go on living after this night, Deirdre, and you with Conchubor in Emain? Are you thinking I'd go out after hares when I've had your lips in my sight?

[Lavarcham comes in as they cling to
   each other.

LAVARCHAM. Are you raving, Deirdre? Are you choosing this night to destroy the world?

DEIRDRE -- very deliberately. -- It's Conchubor has chosen this night calling me to Emain. (To Naisi.) Bring in Ainnle and Ardan, and take me from this place, where I'm in dread from this out of the footsteps of a hare passing. [He goes.

DEIRDRE -- clinging to Lavarcham. -- Do not take it bad I'm going, Lavarcham. It's you have been a good friend and given me great freedom and joy, and I living on Slieve Fuadh; and maybe you'll be well pleased one day saying you have nursed Deirdre.

LAVARCHAM -- moved. -- It isn't I'll be well pleased and I far away from you. Isn't it a hard thing you're doing, but who can help it? Birds go mating in the spring of the year, and ewes at the leaves falling, but a young girl must have her lover in all the courses of the sun and moon.

DEIRDRE. Will you go to Emain in the morning?

LAVARCHAM. I will not. I'll go to Brandon in the south; and in the course of a piece, maybe, I'll be sailing back and forward on the seas to be looking on your face and the little ways you have that none can equal.

[Naisi comes back with Ainnle and Ardan and Old Woman.

DEIRDRE -- taking Naisi's hand. -- My two brothers, I am going with Naisi to Alban and the north to face the troubles are foretold. Will you take word to Conchubor in Emain?

AINNLE. We will go with you.

ARDAN. We will be your servants and your huntsmen, Deirdre.

DEIRDRE. It isn't one brother only of you three is brave and courteous. Will you wed us, Lavarcham? You have the words and customs.

LAVARCHAM. I will not, then. What would I want meddling in the ruin you will earn?

NAISI. Let Ainnle wed us. . . . He has been with wise men and he knows their ways.

AINNLE -- joining their hands. -- By the sun and moon and the whole earth, I wed Deirdre to Naisi. (He steps back and holds up his hands.) May the air bless you, and water and the wind, the sea, and all the hours of the sun and moon.

CURTAIN

ACT II.

Alban. Early morning in the beginning of winter. Outside the tent of Deirdre and Naisi.

Alban. Early morning in the beginning of winter. A wood outside the tent of Deirdre and Naisi. Lavarcham comes in muffled in a cloak.
LAVARCHAM -- calling. -- Deirdre. . . . Deirdre. . . .
DEIRDRE -- coming from tent. -- My welcome, Lavarcham. . . . Whose curagh is rowing from Ulster? I saw the oars through the tops of the trees, and I thought it was you were coming towards us.
LAVARCHAM. I came in the shower was before dawn.
DEIRDRE. And who is coming?
LAVARCHAM -- mournfully. -- Let you not be startled or taking it bad, Deirdre. It's Fergus bringing messages of peace from Conchubor to take Naisi and his brothers back to Emain.   [Sitting down.

DEIRDRE -- lightly. -- Naisi and his brothers are well pleased with this place; and what would take them back to Conchubor in Ulster?

LAVARCHAM. Their like would go any place where they'd see death standing. (With more agitation.) I'm in dread Conchubor wants to have yourself and to kill Naisi, and that that'll be the ruin of the Sons of Usna. I'm silly, maybe, to be dreading the like, but those have a great love for yourself have a right to be in dread always.

DEIRDRE -- more anxiously. -- Emain should be no safe place for myself and Naisi. And isn't it a hard thing they'll leave us no peace, Lavarcham, and we so quiet in the woods?

LAVARCHAM -- impressively. -- It's a hard thing, surely; but let you take my word and swear Naisi, by the earth, and the sun over it, and the four quarters of the moon, he'll not go back to Emain -- for good faith or bad faith -- the time Conchubor's keeping the high throne of Ireland. . . . It's that would save you, surely.

DEIRDRE -- without hope. -- There's little power in oaths to stop what's coming, and little power in what I'd do, Lavarcham, to change the story of Conchubor and Naisi and the things old men foretold.

LAVARCHAM -- aggressively. -- Was there little power in what you did the night you dressed in your finery and ran Naisi off along with you, in spite of Conchubor and the big nobles did dread the blackness of your luck? It was power enough you had that night to bring distress and anguish; and now I'm pointing you a way to save Naisi, you'll not stir stick or straw to aid me.

   DEIRDRE -- a little haughtily. -- Let you not raise your voice against me, Lavarcham, if you have will itself to guard Naisi.

   LAVARCHAM -- breaking out in anger. -- Naisi is it? I didn't care if the crows were stripping his thigh-bones at the dawn of day. It's to stop your own despair and wailing, and you waking up in a cold bed, without the man you have your heart on, I am raging now. (Starting up with temper.) Yet there is more men than Naisi in it; and maybe I was a big fool thinking his dangers, and this day, would fill you up with dread.

   DEIRDRE -- sharply. -- Let you end; such talking is a fool's only, when it's well you know if a thing harmed Naisi it isn't I would live after him. (With distress.) It's well you know it's this day I'm dreading seven years, and I fine nights watching the heifers walking to the haggard with long shadows on the grass; (with emotion) or the time I've been stretched in the sunshine, when I've heard Ainnle and Ardan stepping lightly, and they saying: Was there ever the like of Deirdre for a happy and sleepy queen?

   LAVARCHAM -- not fully pacified. -- And yet you'll go, and welcome is it, if Naisi chooses?

DEIRDRE. I've dread going or staying, Lavarcham. It's lonesome this place, having happiness like ours, till I'm asking each day will this day match yesterday, and will to-morrow take a good place beside the same day in the year that's gone, and wondering all times is it a game worth playing, living on until you're dried and old, and our joy is gone for ever.

LAVARCHAM. If it's that ails you, I tell you there's little hurt getting old, though young girls and poets do be storming at the shapes of age. (Passionately.) There's little hurt getting old, saving when you're looking back, the way I'm looking this day, and seeing the young you have a love for breaking up their hearts with folly. (Going to Deirdre.) Take my word and stop Naisi, and the day'll come you'll have more joy having the senses of an old woman and you with your little grandsons shrieking round you, than I'd have this night putting on the red mouth and the white arms you have, to go walking lonesome byways with a gamey king.

DEIRDRE. It's little joy of a young woman, or an old woman, I'll have from this day, surely. But what use is in our talking when there's Naisi on the foreshore, and Fergus with him?

LAVARCHAM -- despairingly. -- I'm late so with my warnings, for Fergus'd talk the moon over to take a new path in the sky.

(With reproach.) You'll not stop him this day, and isn't it a strange story you were a plague and torment, since you were that height, to those did hang their lifetimes on your voice. (Overcome with trouble; gathering her cloak about her.) Don't think bad of my crying. I'm not the like of many and I'd see a score of naked corpses and not heed them at all, but I'm destroyed seeing yourself in your hour of joy when the end is coming surely.

[Owen comes in quickly, rather ragged, bows to Deirdre.

OWEN -- to Lavarcham. -- Fergus's men are calling you. You were seen on the path, and he and Naisi want you for their talk below.

LAVARCHAM -- looking at him with dislike. -- Yourself's an ill-lucky thing to meet a morning is the like of this. Yet if you are a spy itself I'll go and give my word that's wanting surely. [Goes out.

OWEN -- to Deirdre. -- So I've found you alone, and I after waiting three weeks getting ague and asthma in the chill of the bogs, till I saw Naisi caught with Fergus.

DEIRDRE. I've heard news of Fergus; what brought you from Ulster?

OWEN -- who has been searching, finds a loaf and sits down eating greedily, and cutting it with a large knife. -- The full moon, I'm thinking, and it squeezing the crack in my skull. Was there ever a man crossed nine waves after a fool's wife and he not away in his head?

DEIRDRE -- absently. -- It should be a long time since you left Emain, where there's civility in speech with queens.

OWEN. It's a long while, surely. It's three weeks I am losing my manners beside the Saxon bull-frogs at the head of the bog. Three weeks is a long space, and yet you're seven years spancelled with Naisi and the pair.

DEIRDRE -- beginning to fold up her silks and jewels. -- Three weeks of your days might be long, surely, yet seven years are a short space for the like of Naisi and myself.

OWEN -- derisively. -- If they're a short space there aren't many the like of you. Wasn't there a queen in Tara had to walk out every morning till she'd meet a stranger and see the flame of courtship leaping up within his eye? Tell me now, (leaning towards her) are you well pleased that length with the same man snorting next you at the dawn of day?

DEIRDRE -- very quietly. -- Am I well pleased seven years seeing the same sun throwing light across the branches at the dawn of day? It's a heartbreak to the wise that it's for a short space we have the same things only. (With contempt.) Yet the earth itself is a silly place, maybe, when a man's a fool and talker.

OWEN -- sharply. -- Well, go, take your choice. Stay here and rot with Naisi or go to Conchubor in Emain. Conchubor's a wrinkled fool with a swelling belly on him, and eyes falling downward from his shining crown; Naisi should be stale and weary. Yet there are many roads, Deirdre, and I tell you I'd liefer be bleaching in a bog-hole than living on without a touch of kindness from your eyes and voice. It's a poor thing to be so lonesome you'd squeeze kisses on a cur dog's nose.

   DEIRDRE. Are there no women like yourself could be your friends in Emain?

   OWEN -- vehemently. -- There are none like you, Deirdre. It's for that I'm asking are you going back this night with Fergus?

   DEIRDRE. I will go where Naisi chooses.

   OWEN -- with a burst of rage. -- It's Naisi, Naisi, is it? Then, I tell you, you'll have great sport one day seeing Naisi getting a harshness in his two sheep's eyes and he looking on yourself. Would you credit it, my father used to be in the broom and heather kissing Lavarcham, with a little bird chirping out above their heads, and now she'd scare a raven from a carcase on a hill. (With a sad cry that brings dignity into his voice.) Queens get old, Deirdre, with their white and long arms going from them, and their backs hooping. I tell you it's a poor thing to see a queen's nose reaching down to scrape her chin.

   DEIRDRE -- looking out, a little uneasy. -- Naisi and Fergus are coming on the path.

   OWEN. I'll go so, for if I had you seven years I'd be jealous of the midges and the dust is in the air. (Muffles himself in his cloak; with a sort of warning in his voice.) I'll give you a riddle, Deirdre: Why isn't my father as ugly and old as Conchubor? You've no answer? . . . . It's because Naisi killed him. (With curious expression.) Think of that and you awake at night, hearing Naisi snoring, or the night you hear strange stories of the things I'm doing in Alban or in Ulster either.

    [He goes out, and in a moment Naisi and
       Fergus come in on the other side.

  NAISI -- gaily. -- Fergus has brought messages of peace from Conchubor.

  DEIRDRE -- greeting Fergus. -- He is welcome. Let you rest, Fergus, you should be hot and thirsty after mounting the rocks.

  FERGUS. It's a sunny nook you've found in Alban; yet any man would be well pleased mounting higher rocks to fetch yourself and Naisi back to Emain.

  DEIRDRE -- with keenness. -- They've answered? They would go?

  FERGUS -- benignly. -- They have not, but when I was a young man we'd have given a lifetime to be in Ireland a score of weeks; and to this day the old men have nothing so heavy as knowing it's in a short while they'll lose the high skies are over Ireland, and the lonesome mornings with birds crying on the bogs. Let you come this day, for there's no place but Ireland where the Gael can have peace always.

  NAISI -- gruffly. -- It's true, surely. Yet we're better this place while Conchubor's in

Emain Macha.

FERGUS -- giving him parchments. -- There are your sureties and Conchubor's seal. (To Deirdre.) I am your surety with Conchubor. You'll not be young always, and it's time you were making yourselves ready for the years will come, building up a homely dun beside the seas of Ireland, and getting in your children from the princes' wives. It's little joy wandering till age is on you and your youth is gone away, so you'd best come this night, for you'd have great pleasure putting out your foot and saying, "I am in Ireland, surely."

DEIRDRE. It isn't pleasure I'd have while Conchubor is king in Emain.

FERGUS -- almost annoyed. -- Would you doubt the seals of Conall Cearneach and the kings of Meath? (He gets parchments from his cloak and gives them to Naisi. More gently.) It's easy being fearful and you alone in the woods, yet it would be a poor thing if a timid woman (taunting her a little) could turn away the Sons of Usna from the life of kings. Let you be thinking on the years to come, Deirdre, and the way you'd have a right to see Naisi a high and white-haired justice beside some king of Emain. Wouldn't it be a poor story if a queen the like of you should have no thought but to be scraping up her hours dallying in the sunshine with the sons of kings?

DEIRDRE -- turning away a little haughtily. -- I leave the choice to Naisi. (Turning back towards Fergus.) Yet you'd do well, Fergus, to go on your own way, for the sake of your own years, so you'll not be saying till your hour of death, maybe, it was yourself brought Naisi and his brothers to a grave was scooped by treachery. [Goes into tent.

FERGUS. It is a poor thing to see a queen so lonesome and afraid. (He watches till he is sure Deirdre cannot hear him.) Listen now to what I'm saying. You'd do well to come back to men and women are your match and comrades, and not be lingering until the day that you'll grow weary, and hurt Deirdre showing her the hardness will grow up within your eyes. . . . You're here years and plenty to know it's truth I'm saying.

> [Deirdre comes out of tent with a horn of wine, she catches the beginning of Naisi's speech and stops with stony wonder.

NAISI -- very thoughtfully. -- I'll not tell you a lie. There have been days a while past when I've been throwing a line for salmon or watching for the run of hares, that I've a dread upon me a day'd come I'd weary of her voice, (very slowly) and Deirdre'd see I'd wearied.

FERGUS -- sympathetic but triumphant. -- I knew it, Naisi. . . . And take my word, Deirdre's seen your dread and she'll have no peace from this out in the woods.

NAISI -- with confidence. -- She's not seen it. . . . Deirdre's no thought of getting old or wearied; it's that puts wonder in her days, and she with spirits would keep bravery and laughter in a town with plague.

  [Deirdre drops the horn of wine and
    crouches down where she is.

  FERGUS. That humour'll leave her. But we've no call going too far, with one word borrowing another. Will you come this night to Emain Macha?

  NAISI. I'll not go, Fergus. I've had dreams of getting old and weary, and losing my delight in Deirdre; but my dreams were dreams only. What are Conchubor's seals and all your talk of Emain and the fools of Meath beside one evening in Glen Masain? We'll stay this place till our lives and time are worn out. It's that word you may take in your curagh to Conchubor in Emain.

  FERGUS -- gathering up his parchments. -- And you won't go, surely.

  NAISI. I will not. . . . I've had dread, I tell you, dread winter and summer, and the autumn and the springtime, even when there's a bird in every bush making his own stir till the fall of night; but this talk's brought me ease, and I see we're as happy as the leaves on the young trees, and we'll be so ever and always, though we'd live the age of the eagle and the salmon and the crow of Britain.

  FERGUS -- with anger. -- Where are your brothers? My message is for them also.

  NAISI. You'll see them above chasing otters by the stream.

FERGUS -- bitterly. -- It isn't much I was mistaken, thinking you were hunters only.
  [He goes, Naisi turns towards tent and sees Deirdre crouching down with her cloak round her face. Deirdre comes out.

NAISI. You've heard my words to Fergus? (She does not answer. A pause. He puts his arm round her.) Leave troubling, and we'll go this night to Glen da Ruadh, where the salmon will be running with the tide.   [Crosses and sits down.

DEIRDRE -- in a very low voice. -- With the tide in a little while we will be journeying again, or it is our own blood maybe will be running away. (She turns and clings to him.) The dawn and evening are a little while, the winter and the summer pass quickly, and what way would you and I, Naisi, have joy for ever?

NAISI. We'll have the joy is highest till our age is come, for it isn't Fergus's talk of great deeds could take us back to Emain.

DEIRDRE. It isn't to great deeds you're going but to near troubles, and the shortening of your days the time that they are bright and sunny; and isn't it a poor thing that I, Deirdre, could not hold you away?

NAISI. I've said we'd stay in Alban always.

DEIRDRE. There's no place to stay always. . . . It's a long time we've had, pressing the lips together, going up and down, resting in our arms, Naisi, waking with the smell of June in the tops of the grasses, and listening to the birds in the branches that are highest.... It's a long time we've had, but the end has come, surely.

    NAISI. Would you have us go to Emain, though if any ask the reason we do not know it, and we journeying as the thrushes come from the north, or young birds fly out on a dark sea?

    DEIRDRE. There's reason all times for an end that's come. And I'm well pleased, Naisi, we're going forward in the winter the time the sun has a low place, and the moon has her mastery in a dark sky, for it's you and I are well lodged our last day, where there is a light behind the clear trees, and the berries on the thorns are a red wall.

    NAISI. If our time in this place is ended, come away without Ainnle and Ardan to the woods of the east, for it's right to be away from all people when two lovers have their love only. Come away and we'll be safe always.

    DEIRDRE -- broken-hearted. -- There's no safe place, Naisi, on the ridge of the world. .... And it's in the quiet woods I've seen them digging our grave, throwing out the clay on leaves are bright and withered.

    NAISI -- still more eagerly. -- Come away, Deirdre, and it's little we'll think of safety or the grave beyond it, and we resting in a little corner between the daytime and the long night.

DEIRDRE -- clearly and gravely. -- It's this hour we're between the daytime and a night where there is sleep for ever, and isn't it a better thing to be following on to a near death, than to be bending the head down, and dragging with the feet, and seeing one day a blight showing upon love where it is sweet and tender.

NAISI -- his voice broken with distraction. -- If a near death is coming what will be my trouble losing the earth and the stars over it, and you, Deirdre, are their flame and bright crown? Come away into the safety of the woods.

DEIRDRE -- shaking her head slowly. -- There are as many ways to wither love as there are stars in a night of Samhain; but there is no way to keep life, or love with it, a short space only. . . . It's for that there's nothing lonesome like a love is watching out the time most lovers do be sleeping. . . . It's for that we're setting out for Emain Macha when the tide turns on the sand.

NAISI -- giving in. -- You're right, maybe. It should be a poor thing to see great lovers and they sleepy and old.

DEIRDRE -- with a more tender intensity. -- We're seven years without roughness or growing weary; seven years so sweet and shining, the gods would be hard set to give us seven days the like of them. It's for that we're going to Emain, where there'll be a rest for ever, or a place for forgetting, in great

crowds and they making a stir.
 NAISI -- very softly. -- We'll go, surely, in place of keeping a watch on a love had no match and it wasting away. (They cling to each other for a moment, then Naisi looks up.) There are Fergus and Lavarcham and my two brothers.

> [Deirdre goes. Naisi sits with his head bowed. Owen runs in stealthily, comes behind Naisi and seizes him round the arms. Naisi shakes him off and whips out his sword.

 OWEN -- screaming with derisive laughter and showing his empty hands. -- Ah, Naisi, wasn't it well I didn't kill you that time? There was a fright you got! I've been watching Fergus above -- don't be frightened -- and I've come down to see him getting the cold shoulder, and going off alone.

> [Fergus and others come in. They are all subdued like men at a queen's wake.

 NAISI -- putting up his sword. -- There he is. (Goes to Fergus.) We are going back when the tide turns, I and Deirdre with yourself.
 ALL. Going back!
 AINNLE. And you'll end your life with Deirdre, though she has no match for keeping spirits in a little company is far away by itself?
 ARDAN. It's seven years myself and Ainnle have been servants and bachelors for yourself and Deirdre. Why will you take her back to Conchubor?

NAISI. I have done what Deirdre wishes and has chosen.

FERGUS. You've made a choice wise men will be glad of in the five ends of Ireland.

OWEN. Wise men is it, and they going back to Conchubor? I could stop them only Naisi put in his sword among my father's ribs, and when a man's done that he'll not credit your oath. Going to Conchubor! I could tell of plots and tricks, and spies were well paid for their play. (He throws up a bag of gold.) Are you paid, Fergus?

[He scatters gold pieces over Fergus.

FERGUS. He is raving. . . . Seize him.

OWEN -- flying between them. -- You won't. Let the lot of you be off to Emain, but I'll be off before you. . . . Dead men, dead men! Men who'll die for Deirdre's beauty; I'll be before you in the grave!

[Runs out with his knife in his hand. They all run after him except Lavarcham, who looks out and then clasps her hands. Deirdre comes out to her in a dark cloak.

DEIRDRE. What has happened?

LAVARCHAM. It's Owen's gone raging mad, and he's after splitting his gullet beyond at the butt of the stone. There was ill luck this day in his eye. And he knew a power if he'd said it all.

[Naisi comes back quickly, followed by the others.

AINNLE -- coming in very excited. --

That man knew plots of Conchubor's. We'll not go to Emain, where Conchubor may love her and have hatred for yourself.

FERGUS. Would you mind a fool and raver?

AINNLE. It's many times there's more sense in madmen than the wise. We will not obey Conchubor.

NAISI. I and Deirdre have chosen; we will go back with Fergus.

ARDAN. We will not go back. We will burn your curaghs by the sea.

FERGUS. My sons and I will guard them.

AINNLE. We will blow the horn of Usna and our friends will come to aid us.

NAISI. It is my friends will come.

AINNLE. Your friends will bind your hands, and you out of your wits.

[Deirdre comes forward quickly and comes between Ainnle and Naisi.

DEIRDRE -- in a low voice. -- For seven years the Sons of Usna have not raised their voices in a quarrel.

AINNLE. We will not take you to Emain.

ARDAN. It is Conchubor has broken our peace.

AINNLE -- to Deirdre. -- Stop Naisi going. What way would we live if Conchubor should take you from us?

DEIRDRE. There is no one could take me from you. I have chosen to go back with Fergus. Will you quarrel with me, Ainnle, though I have been your queen these seven years in Alban?

AINNLE -- subsiding suddenly. -- Naisi has no call to take you.

ARDAN. Why are you going?

DEIRDRE -- to both of them and the others. -- It is my wish. . . . It may be I will not have Naisi growing an old man in Alban with an old woman at his side, and young girls pointing out and saying, "that is Deirdre and Naisi had great beauty in their youth." It may be we do well putting a sharp end to the day is brave and glorious, as our fathers put a sharp end to the days of the kings of Ireland; or that I'm wishing to set my foot on Slieve Fuadh, where I was running one time and leaping the streams, (to Lavarcham) and that I'd be well pleased to see our little apple-trees, Lavarcham, behind our cabin on the hill; or that I've learned, Fergus, it's a lonesome thing to be away from Ireland always.

AINNLE -- giving in. -- There is no place but will be lonesome to us from this out, and we thinking on our seven years in Alban.

DEIRDRE -- to Naisi. -- It's in this place we'd be lonesome in the end. . . . Take down Fergus to the sea. He has been a guest had a hard welcome and he bringing messages of peace.

FERGUS. We will make your curagh ready and it fitted for the voyage of a king.

[He goes with Naisi.

DEIRDRE. Take your spears, Ainnle and

Ardan, and go down before me, and take your horse-boys to be carrying my cloaks are on the threshold.

   AINNLE -- obeying. -- It's with a poor heart we'll carry your things this day we have carried merrily so often, and we hungry and cold.

     [They gather up things and go out.

   DEIRDRE -- to Lavarcham. -- Go you, too, Lavarcham. You are old, and I will follow quickly.

   LAVARCHAM. I'm old, surely, and the hopes I had my pride in are broken and torn.

   [She goes out, with a look of awe at
    Deirdre.

   DEIRDRE -- clasping her hands. -- Woods of Cuan, woods of Cuan, dear country of the east! It's seven years we've had a life was joy only, and this day we're going west, this day we're facing death, maybe, and death should be a poor, untidy thing, though it's a queen that dies.

     [She goes out slowly.

CURTAIN

ACT III.

Tent below Emain Macha.

    Tent below Emain, with shabby skins and benches. There is an opening at each side and at back, the latter closed. Old Woman comes in with food and fruits and arranges them on table. Conchubor comes in on right.
    CONCHUBOR -- sharply. -- Has no one come with news for me?
    OLD WOMAN. I've seen no one at all, Conchubor.
    CONCHUBOR -- watches her working for a moment, then makes sure opening at back is closed. -- Go up then to Emain, you're not wanting here. (A noise heard left.) Who is that?
    OLD WOMAN -- going left. -- It's Lavarcham coming again. She's a great wonder for jogging back and forward through the world, and I made certain she'd be off to meet them; but she's coming alone, Conchubor, my dear child Deirdre isn't with her at all.
    CONCHUBOR. Go up so and leave us.

OLD WOMAN -- pleadingly. -- I'd be well pleased to set my eyes on Deirdre if she's coming this night, as we're told.

CONCHUBOR -- impatiently. -- It's not long till you'll see her. But I've matters with Lavarcham, and let you go now, I'm saying.

[He shows her out right, as Lavarcham comes in on the left.

LAVARCHAM -- looking round her with suspicion. -- This is a queer place to find you, and it's a queer place to be lodging Naisi and his brothers, and Deirdre with them, and the lot of us tired out with the long way we have been walking.

CONCHUBOR. You've come along with them the whole journey?

LAVARCHAM. I have, then, though I've no call now to be wandering that length to a wedding or a burial, or the two together. (She sits down wearily.) It's a poor thing the way me and you is getting old, Conchubor, and I'm thinking you yourself have no call to be loitering this place getting your death, maybe, in the cold of night.

CONCHUBOR. I'm waiting only to know is Fergus stopped in the north.

LAVARCHAM -- more sharply. -- He's stopped, surely, and that's a trick has me thinking you have it in mind to bring trouble this night on Emain and Ireland and the big world's east beyond them. (She goes to him.) And yet you'd do well to be going to your dun, and not putting shame on her meeting the High King, and she seamed and sweaty and in great disorder from the dust of many roads. (Laughing derisively.) Ah, Conchubor, my lad, beauty goes quickly in the woods, and you'd let a great gasp, I tell you, if you set your eyes this night on Deirdre.

   CONCHUBOR -- fiercely. -- It's little I care if she's white and worn, for it's I did rear her from a child. I should have a good right to meet and see her always.

   LAVARCHAM. A good right is it? Haven't the blind a good right to be seeing, and the lame to be dancing, and the dummies singing tunes? It's that right you have to be looking for gaiety on Deirdre's lips. (Coaxingly.) Come on to your dun, I'm saying, and leave her quiet for one night itself.

   CONCHUBOR -- with sudden anger. -- I'll not go, when it's long enough I am above in my dun stretching east and west without a comrade, and I more needy, maybe, than the thieves of Meath. . . . You think I'm old and wise, but I tell you the wise know the old must die, and they'll leave no chance for a thing slipping from them they've set their blood to win.

   LAVARCHAM -- nodding her head. -- If you're old and wise, it's I'm the same, Conchubor, and I'm telling you you'll not have her though you're ready to destroy mankind and skin the gods to win her. There's things a king can't have, Conchubor, and if you go rampaging this night you'll be apt to win nothing but death for many, and a sloppy face of trouble on your own self before the day will come.

CONCHUBOR. It's too much talk you have. (Goes right.) Where is Owen? Did you see him no place and you coming the road?

LAVARCHAM. I seen him surely. He went spying on Naisi, and now the worms is spying on his own inside.

CONCHUBOR -- exultingly. -- Naisi killed him?

LAVARCHAM. He did not, then. It was Owen destroyed himself running mad because of Deirdre. Fools and kings and scholars are all one in a story with her like, and Owen thought he'd be a great man, being the first corpse in the game you'll play this night in Emain.

CONCHUBOR. It's yourself should be the first corpse, but my other messengers are coming, men from the clans that hated Usna.

LAVARCHAM -- drawing back hopelessly. -- Then the gods have pity on us all!

[Men with weapons come in.

CONCHUBOR -- to Soldiers. -- Are Ainnle and Ardan separate from Naisi?

MEN. They are, Conchubor. We've got them off, saying they were needed to make ready Deirdre's house.

CONCHUBOR. And Naisi and Deirdre are coming?

SOLDIER. Naisi's coming, surely, and a woman with him is putting out the glory of the moon is rising and the sun is going down.

CONCHUBOR -- looking at Lavarcham. -- That's your story that she's seamed and ugly?

SOLDIER. I have more news. (Pointing to Lavarcham.) When that woman heard you were bringing Naisi this place, she sent a horse-boy to call Fergus from the north.

CONCHUBOR -- to Lavarcham. -- It's for that you've been playing your tricks, but what you've won is a nearer death for Naisi. (To Soldiers.) Go up and call my fighters, and take that woman up to Emain.

LAVARCHAM. I'd liefer stay this place. I've done my best, but if a bad end is coming, surely it would be a good thing maybe I was here to tend her.

CONCHUBOR -- fiercely. -- Take her to Emain; it's too many tricks she's tried this day already. (A Soldier goes to her.)

LAVARCHAM. Don't touch me. (She puts her cloak round her and catches Conchubor's arm.) I thought to stay your hand with my stories till Fergus would come to be beside them, the way I'd save yourself, Conchubor, and Naisi and Emain Macha; but I'll walk up now into your halls, and I'll say (with a gesture) it's here nettles will be growing, and beyond thistles and docks. I'll go into your high chambers, where you've been figuring yourself stretching out your neck for the kisses of a queen of women; and I'll say it's here there'll be deer stirring and goats scratching, and sheep waking and coughing when there is a great wind from the north. (Shaking herself loose. Conchubor makes a sign to Soldiers.) I'm going, surely. In a short space I'll be sitting up with many listening to the flames crackling, and the beams breaking, and I looking on the great blaze will be the end of Emain. [She goes out.

CONCHUBOR -- looking out. -- I see two people in the trees; it should be Naisi and Deirdre. (To Soldier.) Let you tell them they'll lodge here tonight.

[Conchubor goes out right. Naisi and Deirdre come in on left, very weary.

NAISI -- to Soldiers. -- Is it this place he's made ready for myself and Deirdre?

SOLDIER. The Red Branch House is being aired and swept and you'll be called there when a space is by; till then you'd find fruits and drink on this table, and so the gods be with you. [Goes out right.

NAISI -- looking round. -- It's a strange place he's put us camping and we come back as his friends.

DEIRDRE. He's likely making up a welcome for us, having curtains shaken out and rich rooms put in order; and it's right he'd have great state to meet us, and you his sister's son.

NAISI -- gloomily. -- It's little we want with state or rich rooms or curtains, when we're used to the ferns only and cold streams and they making a stir.

DEIRDRE -- roaming round room. -- We want what is our right in Emain (looking at hangings), and though he's riches in store for us it's a shabby, ragged place he's put us waiting, with frayed rugs and skins are eaten by the moths.

NAISI -- a little impatiently. -- There are few would worry over skins and moths on this first night that we've come back to Emain.

DEIRDRE -- brightly. -- You should be well pleased it's for that I'd worry all times, when it's I have kept your tent these seven years as tidy as a bee-hive or a linnet's nest. If Conchubor'd a queen like me in Emain he'd not have stretched these rags to meet us. (She pulls hanging, and it opens.) There's new earth on the ground and a trench dug. . . . It's a grave, Naisi, that is wide and deep.

NAISI -- goes over and pulls back curtain showing grave. -- And that'll be our home in Emain. . . . He's dug it wisely at the butt of a hill, with fallen trees to hide it. He'll want to have us killed and buried before Fergus comes.

DEIRDRE. Take me away. . . . Take me to hide in the rocks, for the night is coming quickly.

NAISI -- pulling himself together. -- I will not leave my brothers.

DEIRDRE -- vehemently. -- It's of us two he's jealous. Come away to the places where we're used to have our company. . . . Wouldn't it be a good thing to lie hid in the high ferns together? (She pulls him left.) I hear strange words in the trees.

NAISI. It should be the strange fighters of Conchubor. I saw them passing as we came.

DEIRDRE -- pulling him towards the right. -- Come to this side. Listen, Naisi!

NAISI. There are more of them. . . . We are shut in, and I have not Ainnle and Ardan to stand near me. Isn't it a hard thing that we three who have conquered many may not die together?

DEIRDRE -- sinking down. -- And isn't it a hard thing that you and I are in this place by our opened grave; though none have lived had happiness like ours those days in Alban that went by so quick.

NAISI. It's a hard thing, surely, we've lost those days for ever; and yet it's a good thing, maybe, that all goes quick, for when I'm in that grave it's soon a day'll come you'll be too wearied to be crying out, and that day'll bring you ease.

DEIRDRE. I'll not be here to know if that is true.

NAISI. It's our three selves he'll kill to-night, and then in two months or three you'll see him walking down for courtship with yourself.

DEIRDRE. I'll not be here.

NAISI -- hard. -- You'd best keep him off, maybe, and then, when the time comes, make your way to some place west in Donegal, and it's there you'll get used to stretching out lonesome at the fall of night, and waking lonesome for the day.

DEIRDRE. Let you not be saying things are worse than death.

NAISI -- a little recklessly. -- I've one word left. If a day comes in the west that the larks are cocking their crests on the edge of the clouds, and the cuckoos making a stir, and there's a man you'd fancy, let you not be thinking that day I'd be well pleased you'd go on keening always.

DEIRDRE -- turning to look at him. -- And if it was I that died, Naisi, would you take another woman to fill up my place?

NAISI -- very mournfully. -- It's little I know, saving only that it's a hard and bitter thing leaving the earth, and a worse and harder thing leaving yourself alone and desolate to be making lamentation on its face always.

DEIRDRE. I'll die when you do, Naisi. I'd not have come here from Alban but I knew I'd be along with you in Emain, and you living or dead. . . . Yet this night it's strange and distant talk you're making only.

NAISI. There's nothing, surely, the like of a new grave of open earth for putting a great space between two friends that love.

DEIRDRE. If there isn't, it's that grave when it's closed will make us one for ever, and we two lovers have had great space without weariness or growing old or any sadness of the mind.

CONCHUBOR -- coming in on right. -- I'd bid you welcome, Naisi.

NAISI -- standing up. -- You're welcome, Conchubor. I'm well pleased you've come.

CONCHUBOR -- blandly. -- Let you not think bad of this place where I've put you till other rooms are readied.

NAISI -- breaking out. -- We know the room you've readied. We know what stirred you to send your seals and Fergus into Alban and stop him in the north, (opening curtain and pointing to the grave) and dig that grave before us. Now I ask what brought you here?

CONCHUBOR. I've come to look on Deirdre.

NAISI. Look on her. You're a knacky fancier, and it's well you chose the one you'd lure from Alban. Look on her, I tell you, and when you've looked I've got ten fingers will squeeze your mottled goose neck, though you're king itself.

DEIRDRE -- coming between them. -- Hush, Naisi! Maybe Conchubor'll make peace.... Do not mind him, Conchubor; he has cause to rage.

CONCHUBOR. It's little I heed his raging, when a call would bring my fighters from the trees.... But what do you say, Deirdre?

DEIRDRE. I'll say so near that grave we seem three lonesome people, and by a new made grave there's no man will keep brooding on a woman's lips, or on the man he hates.

It's not long till your own grave will be dug in Emain, and you'd go down to it more easy if you'd let call Ainnle and Ardan, the way we'd have a supper all together, and fill that grave, and you'll be well pleased from this out, having four new friends the like of us in Emain.

CONCHUBOR -- looking at her for a moment. -- That's the first friendly word I've heard you speaking, Deirdre. A game the like of yours should be the proper thing for softening the heart and putting sweetness in the tongue; and yet this night when I hear you I've small blame left for Naisi that he stole you off from Ulster.

DEIRDRE -- to Naisi. -- Now, Naisi, answer gently, and we'll be friends to-night.

NAISI -- doggedly. -- I have no call but to be friendly. I'll answer what you will.

DEIRDRE -- taking Naisi's hand. -- Then you'll call Conchubor your friend and king, the man who reared me up upon Slieve Fuadh.

[As Conchubor is going to clasp Naisi's hand cries are heard behind.

CONCHUBOR. What noise is that?

AINNLE -- behind. -- Naisi. . . . . Naisi. Come to us; we are betrayed and broken.

NAISI. It's Ainnle crying out in a battle.

CONCHUBOR. I was near won this night, but death's between us now.

[He goes out.

DEIRDRE -- clinging to Naisi. -- There is no battle. . . . Do not leave me, Naisi.

NAISI. I must go to them.

DEIRDRE -- beseechingly. -- Do not leave me, Naisi. Let us creep up in the darkness behind the grave. If there's a battle, maybe the strange fighters will be destroyed, when Ainnle and Ardan are against them.

[Cries heard.

NAISI -- wildly. -- I hear Ardan crying out. Do not hold me from my brothers.

DEIRDRE. Do not leave me, Naisi. Do not leave me broken and alone.

NAISI. I cannot leave my brothers when it is I who have defied the king.

DEIRDRE. I will go with you.

NAISI. You cannot come. Do not hold me from the fight.

[He throws her aside almost roughly.

DEIRDRE -- with restraint. -- Go to your brothers. For seven years you have been kindly, but the hardness of death has come between us.

NAISI -- looking at her aghast. -- And you'll have me meet death with a hard word from your lips in my ear?

DEIRDRE. We've had a dream, but this night has waked us surely. In a little while we've lived too long, Naisi, and isn't it a poor thing we should miss the safety of the grave, and we trampling its edge?

AINNLE -- behind. -- Naisi, Naisi, we are attacked and ruined!

DEIRDRE. Let you go where they are calling. (She looks at him for an instant coldly.) Have you no shame loitering and talking, and a cruel death facing Ainnle and Ardan in the woods?

NAISI -- frantic. -- They'll not get a death that's cruel, and they with men alone. It's women that have loved are cruel only; and if I went on living from this day I'd be putting a curse on the lot of them I'd meet walking in the east or west, putting a curse on the sun that gave them beauty, and on the madder and the stone-crop put red upon their cloaks.

DEIRDRE -- bitterly. -- I'm well pleased there's no one in this place to make a story that Naisi was a laughing-stock the night he died.

NAISI. There'd not be many'd make a story, for that mockery is in your eyes this night will spot the face of Emain with a plague of pitted graves.   [He goes out.

CONCHUBOR -- outside. -- That is Naisi. Strike him! (Tumult. Deirdre crouches down on Naisi's cloak. Conchubor comes in hurriedly.) They've met their death -- the three that stole you, Deirdre, and from this out you'll be my queen in Emain.

[A keen of men's voices is heard behind.

DEIRDRE -- bewildered and terrified. -- It is not I will be a queen.

CONCHUBOR. Make your lamentation a short while if you will, but it isn't long till a day'll come when you begin pitying a man is old and desolate, and High King also. . . . Let you not fear me, for it's I'm well pleased you have a store of pity for the three that were your friends in Alban.

DEIRDRE. I have pity, surely.... It's the way pity has me this night, when I think of Naisi, that I could set my teeth into the heart of a king.

CONCHUBOR. I know well pity's cruel, when it was my pity for my own self destroyed Naisi.

DEIRDRE -- more wildly. -- It was my words without pity gave Naisi a death will have no match until the ends of life and time. (Breaking out into a keen.) But who'll pity Deirdre has lost the lips of Naisi from her neck and from her cheek for ever? Who'll pity Deirdre has lost the twilight in the woods with Naisi, when beech-trees were silver and copper, and ash-trees were fine gold?

CONCHUBOR -- bewildered. -- It's I'll know the way to pity and care you, and I with a share of troubles has me thinking this night it would be a good bargain if it was I was in the grave, and Deirdre crying over me, and it was Naisi who was old and desolate.

[Keen heard.

DEIRDRE -- wild with sorrow. -- It is I who am desolate; I, Deirdre, that will not live till I am old.

CONCHUBOR. It's not long you'll be desolate, and I seven years saying, "It's a bright day for Deirdre in the woods of Alban"; or saying again, "What way will Deirdre be sleeping this night, and wet leaves and branches driving from the north?" Let you not break the thing I've set my life on, and you giving yourself up to your sorrow when it's joy and sorrow do burn out like straw blazing in an east wind.

DEIRDRE -- turning on him. -- Was it that way with your sorrow, when I and Naisi went northward from Slieve Fuadh and let raise our sails for Alban?

CONCHUBOR. There's one sorrow has no end surely -- that's being old and lonesome. (With extraordinary pleading.) But you and I will have a little peace in Emain, with harps playing, and old men telling stories at the fall of night. I've let build rooms for our two selves, Deirdre, with red gold upon the walls and ceilings that are set with bronze. There was never a queen in the east had a house the like of your house, that's waiting for yourself in Emain.

SOLDIER -- running in. -- Emain is in flames. Fergus has come back and is setting fire to the world. Come up, Conchubor, or your state will be destroyed!

CONCHUBOR -- angry and regal again. -- Are the Sons of Usna buried?

SOLDIER. They are in their grave, but no earth is thrown.

CONCHUBOR. Let me see them. Open the tent! (Soldier opens back of tent and shows grave.) Where are my fighters?

SOLDIER. They are gone to Emain.

CONCHUBOR -- to Deirdre. -- There are none to harm you. Stay here until I come again.

> [Goes out with Soldier. Deirdre looks round for a moment, then goes up slowly and looks into grave. She crouches down and begins swaying herself backwards and forwards, keening softly. At first her words are not heard, then they become clear.

DEIRDRE. It's you three will not see age or death coming -- you that were my company when the fires on the hill-tops were put out and the stars were our friends only. I'll turn my thoughts back from this night, that's pitiful for want of pity, to the time it was your rods and cloaks made a little tent for me where there'd be a birch tree making shelter and a dry stone; though from this day my own fingers will be making a tent for me, spreading out my hairs and they knotted with the rain.

> [Lavarcham and Old Woman come in stealthily on right.

DEIRDRE -- not seeing them. -- It is I, Deirdre, will be crouching in a dark place; I, Deirdre, that was young with Naisi, and brought sorrow to his grave in Emain.

OLD WOMAN. Is that Deirdre broken down that was so light and airy?

LAVARCHAM. It is, surely, crying out over their grave. [She goes to Deirdre.

DEIRDRE. It will be my share from this out to be making lamentation on his stone always, and I crying for a love will be the like of a star shining on a little harbour by the sea.

LAVARCHAM -- coming forward. -- Let you rise up, Deirdre, and come off while there are none to heed us, the way I'll find you shelter and some friend to guard you.

DEIRDRE. To what place would I go away from Naisi? What are the woods without Naisi or the sea shore?

LAVARCHAM -- very coaxingly. -- If it is that way you'd be, come till I find you a sunny place where you'll be a great wonder they'll call the queen of sorrows; and you'll begin taking a pride to be sitting up pausing and dreaming when the summer comes.

DEIRDRE. It was the voice of Naisi that was strong in summer -- the voice of Naisi that was sweeter than pipes playing, but from this day will be dumb always.

LAVARCHAM -- to Old Woman. -- She doesn't heed us at all. We'll be hard set to rouse her.

OLD WOMAN. If we don't the High King will rouse her, coming down beside her with the rage of battle in his blood, for how could Fergus stand against him?

LAVARCHAM -- touching Deirdre with her hand. -- There's a score of woman's years in store for you, and you'd best choose will you start living them beside the man you hate, or being your own mistress in the west or south?

DEIRDRE. It is not I will go on living after Ainnle and after Ardan. After Naisi I will not have a lifetime in the world.

OLD WOMAN -- with excitement. -- Look, Lavarcham! There's a light leaving the Red Branch. Conchubor and his lot will be coming quickly with a torch of bog-deal for her marriage, throwing a light on her three comrades.

DEIRDRE -- startled. -- Let us throw down clay on my three comrades. Let us cover up Naisi along with Ainnle and Ardan, they that were the pride of Emain. (Throwing in clay.) There is Naisi was the best of three, the choicest of the choice of many. It was a clean death was your share, Naisi; and it is not I will quit your head, when it's many a dark night among the snipe and plover that you and I were whispering together. It is not I will quit your head, Naisi, when it's many a night we saw the stars among the clear trees of Glen da Ruadh, or the moon pausing to rest her on the edges of the hills.

OLD WOMAN. Conchubor is coming, surely. I see the glare of flames throwing a light upon his cloak.

LAVARCHAM -- eagerly. -- Rise up, Deirdre, and come to Fergus, or be the High King's slave for ever!

DEIRDRE -- imperiously. -- I will not leave Naisi, who has left the whole world scorched and desolate. I will not go away when there is no light in the heavens, and no

flower in the earth under them, but is saying to me that it is Naisi who is gone for ever.

CONCHUBOR -- behind. -- She is here. Stay a little back. (Lavarcham and Old Woman go into the shadow on left as Conchubor comes in. With excitement, to Deirdre.) Come forward and leave Naisi the way I've left charred timber and a smell of burning in Emain Macha, and a heap of rubbish in the storehouse of many crowns.

DEIRDRE -- more awake to what is round her. -- What are crowns and Emain Macha, when the head that gave them glory is this place, Conchubor, and it stretched upon the gravel will be my bed to-night?

CONCHUBOR. Make an end of talk of Naisi, for I've come to bring you to Dundealgan since Emain is destroyed.

 [Conchubor makes a movement towards her.

DEIRDRE -- with a tone that stops him. -- Draw a little back from Naisi, who is young for ever. Draw a little back from the white bodies I am putting under a mound of clay and grasses that are withered -- a mound will have a nook for my own self when the end is come.

CONCHUBOR -- roughly. -- Let you rise up and come along with me in place of growing crazy with your wailings here.

DEIRDRE. It's yourself has made a crazy story, and let you go back to your arms, Conchubor, and to councils where your name is great, for in this place you are an old man and a fool only.

CONCHUBOR. If I've folly, I've sense left not to lose the thing I've bought with sorrow and the deaths of many.

[He moves towards her.

DEIRDRE. Do not raise a hand to touch me.

CONCHUBOR. There are other hands to touch you. My fighters are set round in among the trees.

DEIRDRE. Who'll fight the grave, Conchubor, and it opened on a dark night?

LAVARCHAM -- eagerly. -- There are steps in the wood. I hear the call of Fergus and his men.

CONCHUBOR -- furiously. -- Fergus cannot stop me. I am more powerful than he is, though I am defeated and old.

FERGUS -- comes in to Deirdre; a red glow is seen behind the grove. -- I have destroyed Emain, and now I'll guard you all times, Deirdre, though it was I, without knowledge, brought Naisi to his grave.

CONCHUBOR. It's not you will guard her, for my whole armies are gathering. Rise up, Deirdre, for you are mine surely.

FERGUS -- coming between them. -- I am come between you.

CONCHUBOR -- wildly. -- When I've killed Naisi and his brothers, is there any man that I will spare? And is it you will stand against me, Fergus, when it's seven years you've seen me getting my death with rage in Emain?

FERGUS. It's I, surely, will stand against a thief and a traitor.

DEIRDRE -- stands up and sees the light from Emain. -- Draw a little back with the squabbling of fools when I am broken up with misery. (She turns round.) I see the flames of Emain starting upward in the dark night; and because of me there will be weasels and wild cats crying on a lonely wall where there were queens and armies and red gold, the way there will be a story told of a ruined city and a raving king and a woman will be young for ever. (She looks round.) I see the trees naked and bare, and the moon shining. Little moon, little moon of Alban, it's lonesome you'll be this night, and tomorrow night, and long nights after, and you pacing the woods beyond Glen Laoi, looking every place for Deirdre and Naisi, the two lovers who slept so sweetly with each other.

FERGUS -- going to Conchubor's right and whispering. -- Keep back, or you will have the shame of pushing a bolt on a queen who is out of her wits.

CONCHUBOR. It is I who am out of my wits, with Emain in flames, and Deirdre raving, and my own heart gone within me.

DEIRDRE -- in a high and quiet tone. -- I have put away sorrow like a shoe that is worn out and muddy, for it is I have had a life that will be envied by great companies. It was not by a low birth I made kings uneasy, and they sitting in the halls of Emain. It was not a low thing to be chosen by Conchubor, who was wise, and Naisi had no match for bravery. It is not a small thing to be rid of grey hairs, and the loosening of the teeth. (With a sort of triumph.) It was the choice of lives we had in the clear woods, and in the grave, we're safe, surely. . . .

CONCHUBOR. She will do herself harm.

DEIRDRE -- showing Naisi's knife. -- I have a little key to unlock the prison of Naisi you'd shut upon his youth for ever. Keep back, Conchubor; for the High King who is your master has put his hands between us. (She half turns to the grave.) It was sorrows were foretold, but great joys were my share always; yet it is a cold place I must go to be with you, Naisi; and it's cold your arms will be this night that were warm about my neck so often. . . . It's a pitiful thing to be talking out when your ears are shut to me. It's a pitiful thing, Conchubor, you have done this night in Emain; yet a thing will be a joy and triumph to the ends of life and time.

   [She presses knife into her heart and
      sinks into the grave. Conchubor and
      Fergus go forward. The red glow
      fades, leaving stage very dark.

FERGUS. Four white bodies are laid down together; four clear lights are quenched in Ireland. (He throws his sword into the grave.) There is my sword that could not shield you -- my four friends that were the dearest always. The flames of Emain have gone out: Deirdre is dead and there is none to keen her. That is the fate of Deirdre and the children of Usna, and for this night, Conchubor, our war is ended. [He goes out.

LAVARCHAM. I have a little hut where you can rest, Conchubor; there is a great dew falling.

CONCHUBOR -- with the voice of an old man. -- Take me with you. I'm hard set to see the way before me.

OLD WOMAN. This way, Conchubor.
 [They go out.

LAVARCHAM -- beside the grave. -- Deirdre is dead, and Naisi is dead; and if the oaks and stars could die for sorrow, it's a dark sky and a hard and naked earth we'd have this night in Emain.

CURTAIN

www.bookjungle.com *email: sales@bookjungle.com fax: 630-214-0564 mail: Book Jungle PO Box 2226 Champaign, IL 61825*

The Codes Of Hammurabi And Moses
W. W. Davies

QTY

The discovery of the Hammurabi Code is one of the greatest achievements of archaeology, and is of paramount interest, not only to the student of the Bible, but also to all those interested in ancient history...

Religion   **ISBN:** *1-59462-338-4*   Pages:132
MSRP *$12.95*

The Theory of Moral Sentiments
Adam Smith

QTY

This work from 1749. contains original theories of conscience amd moral judgment and it is the foundation for systemof morals.

Philosophy   ISBN: *1-59462-777-0*   Pages:536
MSRP *$19.95*

Jessica's First Prayer
Hesba Stretton

QTY

In a screened and secluded corner of one of the many railway-bridges which span the streets of London there could be seen a few years ago, from five o'clock every morning until half past eight, a tidily set-out coffee-stall, consisting of a trestle and board, upon which stood two large tin cans, with a small fire of charcoal burning under each so as to keep the coffee boiling during the early hours of the morning when the work-people were thronging into the city on their way to their daily toil...

Childrens   **ISBN:** *1-59462-373-2*   Pages:84
MSRP *$9.95*

My Life and Work
Henry Ford

QTY

Henry Ford revolutionized the world with his implementation of mass production for the Model T automobile. Gain valuable business insight into his life and work with his own auto-biography... "We have only started on our development of our country we have not as yet, with all our talk of wonderful progress, done more than scratch the surface. The progress has been wonderful enough but..."

Biographies/   **ISBN:** *1-59462-198-5*   Pages:300
MSRP *$21.95*

www.bookjungle.com email: sales@bookjungle.com fax: 630-214-0564 mail: Book Jungle PO Box 2226 Champaign, IL 61825

The Art of Cross-Examination
Francis Wellman

QTY

I presume it is the experience of every author, after his first book is published upon an important subject, to be almost overwhelmed with a wealth of ideas and illustrations which could readily have been included in his book, and which to his own mind, at least, seem to make a second edition inevitable. Such certainly was the case with me; and when the first edition had reached its sixth impression in five months, I rejoiced to learn that it seemed to my publishers that the book had met with a sufficiently favorable reception to justify a second and considerably enlarged edition. ..

Reference   ISBN: *1-59462-647-2*

Pages: 412
MSRP $19.95

On the Duty of Civil Disobedience
Henry David Thoreau

QTY

Thoreau wrote his famous essay, On the Duty of Civil Disobedience, as a protest against an unjust but popular war and the immoral but popular institution of slave-owning. He did more than write—he declined to pay his taxes, and was hauled off to gaol in consequence. Who can say how much this refusal of his hastened the end of the war and of slavery?

Law   ISBN: *1-59462-747-9*

Pages: 48
MSRP $7.45

Dream Psychology Psychoanalysis for Beginners
Sigmund Freud

QTY

Sigmund Freud, born Sigismund Schlomo Freud (May 6, 1856 - September 23, 1939), was a Jewish-Austrian neurologist and psychiatrist who co-founded the psychoanalytic school of psychology. Freud is best known for his theories of the unconscious mind, especially involving the mechanism of repression; his redefinition of sexual desire as mobile and directed towards a wide variety of objects; and his therapeutic techniques, especially his understanding of transference in the therapeutic relationship and the presumed value of dreams as sources of insight into unconscious desires.

Psychology   ISBN: *1-59462-905-6*

Pages: 196
MSRP $15.45

The Miracle of Right Thought
Orison Swett Marden

QTY

Believe with all of your heart that you will do what you were made to do. When the mind has once formed the habit of holding cheerful, happy, prosperous pictures, it will not be easy to form the opposite habit. It does not matter how improbable or how far away this realization may see, or how dark the prospects may be, if we visualize them as best we can, as vividly as possible, hold tenaciously to them and vigorously struggle to attain them, they will gradually become actualized, realized in the life. But a desire, a longing without endeavor, a yearning abandoned or held indifferently will vanish without realization.

Self Help   ISBN: *1-59462-644-8*

Pages: 360
MSRP $25.45

www.bookjungle.com email: sales@bookjungle.com fax: 630-214-0564 mail: Book Jungle PO Box 2226 Champaign, IL 61825

QTY

	Title	ISBN	Price
☐	**The Rosicrucian Cosmo-Conception Mystic Christianity** *by Max Heindel* *The Rosicrucian Cosmo-conception is not dogmatic, neither does it appeal to any other authority than the reason of the student. It is: not controversial, but is: sent forth in the, hope that it may help to clear...* New Age/Religion Pages 646	ISBN: *1-59462-188-8*	**$38.95**
☐	**Abandonment To Divine Providence** *by Jean-Pierre de Caussade* *"The Rev. Jean Pierre de Caussade was one of the most remarkable spiritual writers of the Society of Jesus in France in the 18th Century. His death took place at Toulouse in 1751. His works have gone through many editions and have been republished...* Inspirational/Religion Pages 400	ISBN: *1-59462-228-0*	**$25.95**
☐	**Mental Chemistry** *by Charles Haanel* *Mental Chemistry allows the change of material conditions by combining and appropriately utilizing the power of the mind. Much like applied chemistry creates something new and unique out of careful combinations of chemicals the mastery of mental chemistry...* New Age Pages 354	ISBN: *1-59462-192-6*	**$23.95**
☐	**The Letters of Robert Browning and Elizabeth Barret Barrett 1845-1846 vol II** *by Robert Browning and Elizabeth Barrett* Biographies Pages 596	ISBN: *1-59462-193-4*	**$35.95**
☐	**Gleanings In Genesis (volume I)** *by Arthur W. Pink* *Appropriately has Genesis been termed "the seed plot of the Bible" for in it we have, in germ form, almost all of the great doctrines which are afterwards fully developed in the books of Scripture which follow...* Religion/Inspirational Pages 420	ISBN: *1-59462-130-6*	**$27.45**
☐	**The Master Key** *by L. W. de Laurence* *In no branch of human knowledge has there been a more lively increase of the spirit of research during the past few years than in the study of Psychology, Concentration and Mental Discipline. The requests for authentic lessons in Thought Control, Mental Discipline and...* New Age/Business Pages 422	ISBN: *1-59462-001-6*	**$30.95**
☐	**The Lesser Key Of Solomon Goetia** *by L. W. de Laurence* *This translation of the first book of the "Lemegton" which is now for the first time made accessible to students of Talismanic Magic was done, after careful collation and edition, from numerous Ancient Manuscripts in Hebrew, Latin, and French...* New Age/Occult Pages 92	ISBN: *1-59462-092-X*	**$9.95**
☐	**Rubaiyat Of Omar Khayyam** *by Edward Fitzgerald* *Edward Fitzgerald, whom the world has already learned, in spite of his own efforts to remain within the shadow of anonymity, to look upon as one of the rarest poets of the century, was born at Bredfield, in Suffolk, on the 31st of March, 1809. He was the third son of John Purcell...* Music Pages 172	ISBN: *1-59462-332-5*	**$13.95**
☐	**Ancient Law** *by Henry Maine* *The chief object of the following pages is to indicate some of the earliest ideas of mankind, as they are reflected in Ancient Law, and to point out the relation of those ideas to modern thought.* Religion/History Pages 452	ISBN: *1-59462-128-4*	**$29.95**
☐	**Far-Away Stories** *by William J. Locke* *"Good wine needs no bush,' but a collection of mixed vintages does. And this book is just such a collection. Some of the stories I do not want to remain buried for ever in the museum files of dead magazine-numbers an author's not unpardonable vanity..."* Fiction Pages 272	ISBN: *1-59462-129-2*	**$19.45**
☐	**Life of David Crockett** *by David Crockett* *"Colonel David Crockett was one of the most remarkable men of the times in which he lived. Born in humble life, but gifted with a strong will, an indomitable courage, and unremitting perseverance...* Biographies/New Age Pages 424	ISBN: *1-59462-250-7*	**$27.45**
☐	**Lip-Reading** *by Edward Nitchie* *Edward B. Nitchie, founder of the New York School for the Hard of Hearing, now the Nitchie School of Lip-Reading, Inc, wrote "LIP-READING Principles and Practice". The development and perfecting of this meritorious work on lip-reading was an undertaking...* How-to Pages 400	ISBN: *1-59462-206-X*	**$25.95**
☐	**A Handbook of Suggestive Therapeutics, Applied Hypnotism, Psychic Science** *by Henry Munro* Health/New Age/Health/Self-help Pages 376	ISBN: *1-59462-214-0*	**$24.95**
☐	**A Doll's House: and Two Other Plays** *by Henrik Ibsen* *Henrik Ibsen created this classic when in revolutionary 1848 Rome. Introducing some striking concepts in playwriting for the realist genre, this play has been studied the world over.* Fiction/Classics/Plays 308	ISBN: *1-59462-112-8*	**$19.95**
☐	**The Light of Asia** *by sir Edwin Arnold* *In this poetic masterpiece, Edwin Arnold describes the life and teachings of Buddha. The man who was to become known as Buddha to the world was born as Prince Gautama of India but he rejected the worldly riches and abandoned the reigns of power when...* Religion/History/Biographies Pages 170	ISBN: *1-59462-204-3*	**$13.95**
☐	**The Complete Works of Guy de Maupassant** *by Guy de Maupassant* *"For days and days, nights and nights, I had dreamed of that first kiss which was to consecrate our engagement, and I knew not on what spot I should put my lips..."* Fiction/Classics Pages 240	ISBN: *1-59462-157-8*	**$16.95**
☐	**The Art of Cross-Examination** *by Francis L. Wellman* *Written by a renowned trial lawyer, Wellman imparts his experience and uses case studies to explain how to use psychology to extract desired information through questioning.* How-to/Science/Reference Pages 408	ISBN: *1-59462-309-0*	**$26.95**
☐	**Answered or Unanswered?** *by Louisa Vaughan* *Miracles of Faith in China* Religion Pages 112	ISBN: *1-59462-248-5*	**$10.95**
☐	**The Edinburgh Lectures on Mental Science (1909)** *by Thomas* *This book contains the substance of a course of lectures recently given by the writer in the Queen Street Hall, Edinburgh. Its purpose is to indicate the Natural Principles governing the relation between Mental Action and Material Conditions...* New Age/Psychology Pages 148	ISBN: *1-59462-008-3*	**$11.95**
☐	**Ayesha** *by H. Rider Haggard* *Verily and indeed it is the unexpected that happens! Probably if there was one person upon the earth from whom the Editor of this, and of a certain previous history, did not expect to hear again...* Classics Pages 380	ISBN: *1-59462-301-5*	**$24.95**
☐	**Ayala's Angel** *by Anthony Trollope* *The two girls were both pretty, but Lucy who was twenty-one who supposed to be simple and comparatively unattractive, whereas Ayala was credited, as her Bombwhat romantic name might show, with poetic charm and a taste for romance. Ayala when her father died was nineteen...* Fiction Pages 484	ISBN: *1-59462-352-X*	**$29.95**
☐	**The American Commonwealth** *by James Bryce* *An interpretation of American democratic political theory. It examines political mechanics and society from the perspective of Scotsman James Bryce.* Politics Pages 572	ISBN: *1-59462-286-8*	**$34.45**
☐	**Stories of the Pilgrims** *by Margaret P. Pumphrey* *This book explores pilgrims religious oppression in England as well as their escape to Holland and eventual crossing to America on the Mayflower, and their early days in New England...* History Pages 268	ISBN: *1-59462-116-0*	**$17.95**

www.bookjungle.com *email: sales@bookjungle.com fax: 630-214-0564 mail: Book Jungle PO Box 2226 Champaign, IL 61825*

QTY

The Fasting Cure *by Sinclair Upton*   ISBN: *1-59462-222-1*   **$13.95**
In the Cosmopolitan Magazine for May, 1910, and in the Contemporary Review (London) for April, 1910, I published an article dealing with my experiences in fasting. I have written a great many magazine articles, but never one which attracted so much attention... New Age/Self Help/Health Pages 164

Hebrew Astrology *by Sepharial*   ISBN: *1-59462-308-2*   **$13.45**
In these days of advanced thinking it is a matter of common observation that we have left many of the old landmarks behind and that we are now pressing forward to greater heights and to a wider horizon than that which represented the mind-content of our progenitors... Astrology Pages 144

Thought Vibration or The Law of Attraction in the Thought World   ISBN: *1-59462-127-6*   **$12.95**
by William Walker Atkinson   Psychology/Religion Pages 144

Optimism *by Helen Keller*   ISBN: *1-59462-108-X*   **$15.95**
Helen Keller was blind, deaf, and mute since 19 months old, yet famously learned how to overcome these handicaps, communicate with the world, and spread her lectures promoting optimism. An inspiring read for everyone... Biographies/Inspirational Pages 84

Sara Crewe *by Frances Burnett*   ISBN: *1-59462-360-0*   **$9.45**
In the first place, Miss Minchin lived in London. Her home was a large, dull, tall one, in a large, dull square, where all the houses were alike, and all the sparrows were alike, and where all the door-knockers made the same heavy sound... Childrens/Classic Pages 88

The Autobiography of Benjamin Franklin *by Benjamin Franklin*   ISBN: *1-59462-135-7*   **$24.95**
The Autobiography of Benjamin Franklin has probably been more extensively read than any other American historical work, and no other book of its kind has had such ups and downs of fortune. Franklin lived for many years in England, where he was agent... Biographies/History Pages 332

Name	
Email	
Telephone	
Address	
City, State ZIP	

☐ Credit Card   ☐ Check / Money Order

Credit Card Number	
Expiration Date	
Signature	

Please Mail to: Book Jungle
PO Box 2226
Champaign, IL 61825
or Fax to: 630-214-0564

ORDERING INFORMATION

web: *www.bookjungle.com*
email: *sales@bookjungle.com*
fax: *630-214-0564*
mail: *Book Jungle PO Box 2226 Champaign, IL 61825*
or PayPal *to sales@bookjungle.com*

Please contact us for bulk discounts

DIRECT-ORDER TERMS

**20% Discount if You Order
Two or More Books**
Free Domestic Shipping!
Accepted: Master Card, Visa,
Discover, American Express

www.ingramcontent.com/pod-product-compliance
Lightning Source LLC
Chambersburg PA
CBHW081327040426
42453CB00013B/2319